TRAVAIL

THE PANT OF GOD AND THE RIGHTEOUS

NIKKI GARCIA

ISBN-13: 979-8-89587-247-5
Cover design by Nikki Garcia
Copyright Case Number: 1-14299028781
Printed in the United States of America

DEDICATION

5 I am the true vine, and my Father is the husbandman.

2 Every branch in me that beareth not fruit he taketh away: and every branch that beareth fruit, he purgeth it, that it may bring forth more fruit.

This book is dedicated to all the branches connected to the true vine. May you always bear much fruit.

CONTENTS

ACKNOWLEDGMENTS

I would like to acknowledge my Lord and Savior, Jesus Christ, the anointed one, the Holy One of Israel, and the soon-coming King, for giving me the revelations in this book. I also want to acknowledge my husband and family for their undying support.

INTRODUCTION

It is so funny how God chooses to speak to us. He is so unique in the way He speaks! I had been traversing through how to start this book. I knew how to do this manner of prayer, but how do I explain this to God's Ekklesia? I had taught on travail only once during an evangelistic event my mother had. I had yet to learn more about this manner of prayer beyond the studies and information I collected from that study. One of my friends □, a believer in Christ and a prophet of the Lord, texted me this love note from God:

"I had a dream last night with you in it. We were talking about how you ascend in prayer to literal places and things change. You were unsure how you got there or how to work it. But you were being observed by some influential people who had taken notice. In the dream, I saw you trying to understand it and make it make sense. But it was travail and supplication. Hope this helps something.□"

Then, God took me on this journey one night. I call this type of surfing going down the rabbit hole. I was studying the prayer of supplication. I didn't know about it and wanted to gain knowledge of it. I had asked a few people what the Prayer of Supplication meant to them, and there were many varied answers, so I went on a biblical trace from Hebrew to English to figure things out. Out of this research, I came up with some very insightful understanding, and this book will reveal that understanding, along with previous experiential knowledge and studies on the prayer of travail and how it traverses varying types of prayer to its ascent.

THE TRAVAIL OF GOD THE FATHER

THE PANT OF GOD

THE TRAVAIL OF GOD THE FATHER
Introducing Travail

Have you ever noticed that before some major weather shift occurs, one of two things happens: there is either a dead stillness, and then boom, something significant happens, or there is a wind ushering in a shift?

In Genesis 1:2, it reads as follows:

[2] And the earth was without form, and void; and darkness was upon the face of the deep. And the Spirit of God moved upon the face of the waters.

One can observe one of the major shifts that occurred by reviewing the word "moved" in the above Scripture. In Hebrew, that word is rachaph.

This word means "brood." An example of brooding is a mother hen and her chicken coop. When the mother hen lays her eggs, she sits on top of them to hatch them. This is what brooding is. This type of brooding is interchangeable with the word "travail."

The Spirit of God brooded over the waters, and He began to birth forth from this place. According to the book of Genesis, God said, saw, and called. Over the next six days, He would birth a new beginning, a place for mankind. Through this brooding, there was an ushering of a major shift on the earth and in heaven.

According to Medical News Today, isn't it interesting that science tells us that 45-75% of our bodies are made up of water, and this is where God started when He began to give birth? Think about this as well: according to WebMD, when a woman gives birth, the baby comes out of amniotic fluid, which is 98% water.

My point in mentioning these considerations is that God

birthed out of the waters. The waters are life-sustaining. As God was creating, He was travailing. That is what brooding is. It is depicted by the travail of God over the waters by His Spirit. Imagine it this way: Earth was the womb, the womb had a placenta, the waters in the placenta represent the amniotic fluid in a woman's placenta, and out of the waters came some of the things God chose to birth forth.

We can see God created it, but the waters gave birth in the following scriptures:

Genesis 1:20-21
*[20] And God said, **Let the waters bring forth abundantly the moving creature that hath life, and fowl that may fly above the earth in the open firmament of heaven.** [21] **And God created great whales, and every living creature that moveth, which the waters brought forth abundantly,** after their kind, and every winged fowl after his kind: and God saw that it was good.*

The Hebrew word "bring forth" in verse 20 is *sharats*. It means to swarm or to teem. The waters were swarming with life. The New American Standard Bible defines this as "to breed abundantly."

One thing we can observe as we read how God created in the Book of Genesis is that God had many ways that He created. Even in creation, He was unique. We can see a pattern in His creation by observing the words He used while in the travail of creating. Those words include: form, shape, make, and saying.

We will delve into the 3 patterns of creating below: create, shape, and form.

CREATE. SHAPE. FORM.

The imagination is where ideas are framed. The heart of man is where the intent, motives, and actions form what was framed in the imagination.

Here is an excerpt from my book 4D Love that explains this further

"The heart is depicted as an exceedingly deep place, characterized by the moanings and groanings akin to Jesus in the Garden of Gethsemane. This deep place of travail represents great intimacy—a place where moanings lead to the formation of Christ within, shaping believers into the very character of God and allowing them to shun the mere appearance of evil. This deep place is where one progresses from being a child of God to becoming His bride."

From the above passage, you can observe travail being associated with moanings and groanings. You can also observe how forming happens: that Christ be formed in a believer.

Galatians 4:19
19 My little children, of whom I travail in birth again until Christ be formed in you,

We will touch more on the travail of redemption in a later chapter, but let's delve further into creation to gather more information that will assist in understanding the travail associated with it.

CREATE
The Creation of Heaven and Earth

The book of Genesis explains genealogy, which is confirmed by the Scripture below.

Genesis 2:4 KJV
[4] These are the generations of the heavens and of the earth when they were created, in the day that the LORD God made the earth and the heavens,

Genesis 1:1 starts like this: In the beginning. This reveals a moment in time. It reveals a new now. This was the start of something new.

1 In the beginning God created the heaven and the earth.

Then it goes on to say, "God." This reveals that this new now starts with God and He is the head of this movement. The scripture proceeds to say, "**created** the heaven and the earth". From this portion of scripture, we delve into the offspring of God. From God comes the heaven and the earth. The root is God and the offspring is the heaven and the earth.

2 And the earth was without form, and void; and darkness was upon the face of the deep. And the Spirit of God moved upon the face of the waters.
3 And God said, Let there be light: and there was light.

God continues to create the atmosphere and dwelling place of this new dimension called earth.

He goes on to say, "Let there be light." This is indicative of the establishment of a type of comprehension. One thing we know about this dimension scientifically is that there are different types of light waves, and as residents of earth, we are able to comprehend light waves. That comprehension allows us to see on earth's frequency. For instance, bees see ultraviolet rays, also known as UV rays, while humans see a small portion of the electromagnetic spectrum called visible light. This is the light of the living, but this is not the only interpretation of light. This is the interpretation of a lesser glory here on earth, but we have an inherent ability as born-again beings to interpret the light of His presence. This illuminates our understanding at varied degrees.

Psalms 56:14 *says it this way*
For you rescued me from death, you kept my feet from stumbling, so that I can walk in God's presence, in the light of life.

Continuing on with the offspring of heaven and earth.

Psalms 33:6-9
*[6] By the word of the LORD were the heavens made; And all the host of them by the **breath of his mouth**. [7] He gathereth the waters of the sea together as an heap: He layeth up the depth in storehouses. [8] Let all the earth fear the LORD: Let all the inhabitants of the world stand in awe of him. [9] **For he spake, and it was done; He commanded, and it stood fast**.*

Let's examine verse 6, which says, "by the breath of his mouth." This is the very breath used in the creation of man; when God breathed into the nostrils of man, he became a living soul.

I would like to take this time to recount a moment of prayer when God was showing me how things appear from the invisible realm into this visible realm. I saw sparkles of light that turned into the actual object on earth.

Let's review a Scripture from the book of Hebrews to explore how our invisible breath causes things to appear on earth.

Hebrews 11:3 KJV
[3] Through faith we understand that the worlds were framed by the word of God, so that things which are seen were not made of things which do appear.

Now let's review the breath of God in the book of Genesis.

Genesis 2:7 KJV
[7] And the LORD God formed man of the dust of the ground, and breathed into his nostrils the breath of life; and man became a living soul.

The Hebrew word for breath is ruach. It means breath, wind, or spirit.

His breath is the driving force of life but here we have the **pant of God.** By his breath, everything was created. That was God's labor, His work, His Travail.

HOW DOES MAN CREATE LIKE GOD?

Exercise 1: Unlock your imagination

Matthew 18:3
And said, Verily I say unto you, Except ye be converted, and become as little children, ye shall not enter into the kingdom of heaven.

My husband told my 11-year-old son to clean up his toys on the dining room table. My son went into his room, got the container for the toys, and automatically entered imagination land. As he was putting the toys in the container, he began to make animated sounds. He pushed them off the table, and they fell into the container.

As I sat there watching and listening to him dive into the world of imagination, I had a eureka moment and thought, "That's it! We have to remain childlike and continue, even as adults, to imagine; that we can receive from the supernatural Kingdom of God and produce heaven on Earth."

Exercise 1a: When you hear the word "Kingdom," what comes to your imagination? Write it below.

Exercise 1b: When you think of the throne of God, what comes to your imagination? Write it below.

Expertise 1c: Let's read this passage of Scripture

Revelation 4:2-5 KJV
[2] And immediately I was in the spirit: and, behold, a throne was set in heaven, and one sat on the throne. [3] And he that sat was to look upon like a jasper and a sardine stone: and there was a rainbow round about the throne, in sight like unto an emerald. [4] And round about the throne were four and twenty seats: and upon the seats I saw four and twenty elders

sitting, clothed in white raiment; and they had on their heads crowns of gold. [5] And out of the throne proceeded lightnings and thunderings and voices: and there were seven lamps of fire burning before the throne, which are the seven Spirits of God.

Draw what you just read. It doesn't matter if you can draw well or not. The objective is to get use to seeing in the spirit.

Let's look at Jeremiah 15:9 in two different translations to compare symbols. Version 1 is the King James Version (KJV) and version 2 is the New American Standard Bible (NAS).

KJV: Jeremiah 15:9
[9] She that hath borne seven languisheth: she hath given up the ghost;

According to Webster, "languisheth" means to be or become

feeble, weak, or to deteriorate.

In the translation of the KJV, this woman has completed the work of birthing forth. She birthed 7 children. The woman becomes weak and passes away.

NAS: [sons] pines away; Her breathing is labored.

I love the NAS translation because it puts things into perspective. Let's focus on the part of Scripture that says, "Her breathing is labored." In the travail of God, His work and His labor were His breathing, and the very breath that was connected to the words that He spoke. In this Scripture, we can pictorially see how this woman is transitioning to death and how her breath is coming to the end of its work.

By combining these two versions of this one Scripture, one can surmise that breathing and birthing are connected, and as long as you are living, birthing takes place. Our words are the seed, and the breath is the transport system used to connect to the ghost or the spirit of God in man that brings life to the words we speak.

John 7:38 KJV
[38] He that believeth on me, as the scripture hath said, out of his belly shall flow rivers of living water.

From the above Scripture, one can see that the belly is where the spirit flows. The belly is the womb of the Spirit. Out of that womb flows water, and the water brings forth that which is living. This is how the transport system I spoke of earlier works. This transport system allows us to bring forth from the unseen realm to the seen realm.

As God continued to create in Scripture, we see that the word says, "and God saw that it was good." This further confirms that there was transport from the invisible to the visible because the word says He saw. What He created was no longer invisible but was now visible.

Exercise 2: Imagine a garden. Now imagine it has nothing in it, and you are walking around. The garden signifies your life. Look into your life and see what you may need to plant. Now find a Scripture and speak that which is missing into existence according to God's word.

SHAPE

As I began to write this section my fingers began to do an outline of something over and over again. This is how "shape" works. Think about how we bake. You mix water and flour together, and at first, the mixture is just a glob of two separate substances. There is no shape; it is invisible, only hoped for. Through our hope and imagination, we create, in this womb, what we want this substance to become. If one wants to make cookies, one may get metal shapers which are the outline(s) for the shape we want the mixture to form into.

One would press the metal shaper onto the dough and the dough now takes on the shape of what we are trying to create.

Let's read **Genesis 1:21**.

21 And God created great whales, and every living creature that moveth, which the waters brought forth abundantly, after their kind, and every winged fowl after his kind: and God saw that it was good.

The word created in verse 21 is the Hebrew word bara. The

word bara means to shape. God created it. He shaped what He was creating, but the waters brought what He shaped in abundance.

We can examine the definition below from bible study tools.

bara': choose

Original Word: בָּ רָ א

Part of Speech: Verb
Transliteration: bara'
Phonetic Spelling: (baw-raw')
Definition: to shape, create

So far, we have reviewed 2 different ways God chose to create: with His breath and through shaping.

This same Hebrew word, bara, is used in Psalm 51:5, which is a prayer of repentance that King David prayed for his infamous sin against Bathsheba.

Psalm 51:5 KJV
[5] Behold, I was shapen in iniquity; And in sin did my mother conceive me.

If you know the story of David, then you know that David had a son with Bathsheba. The son, as the Scripture says, he was shapen in iniquity. Now, what does that mean?

We're going to focus on two aspects of this Scripture.

(1)   *"I was **shapen in iniquity**"*
First, let's define iniquity. According to Webster, iniquity is defined as gross injustice or wickedness.

From this definition, one can see how David's continual actions were multiple violations against the marital covenant of Uriah and Bathsheba, culminating in the death of her spouse. It was gross injustice. This iniquitous situation was shaped by David's knowledge, understanding, thoughts, intents, and actions. Out of this heart of wickedness came the child named Solomon.

(2)   *"in sin did my mother **conceive** me"*
The word "conceive" is yacham in Hebrew, and it means to be hot or to conceive. It is literally used in the act of conceiving in animals. In essence, this baby was conceived out of the lust of the flesh; it was a burning desire.

We even see this concept today in education. If you observe school slogans, some mirror this thought: "Shaping the minds of our young people." Through knowledge and understanding, our educational systems shape the minds of our children to adapt to their teachings.

One last example of shape is the Hebrew language. It is filled with shapes. The shapes utilized in their language has rich meaning. One symbol can have 3 or more meanings, making this language rich in intent and pursuit.

HOW DOES MAN SHAPE AS GOD DID?

In summary, man shapes as God did, through intent and pursuit. When we take the knowledge and understanding we have, we choose whether we will birth in righteousness or iniquity. The outline of what is created is encapsulated in the heart of man, and out of the abundance of our inner desires, what we create is shaped.

THE SHAPE ENCOUNTER

After a long week, I finally got the chance to put the prayers I shaped into the sea. They were outlines, as it were, of the things I wanted to bring forth in abundance. I drew them on notepads. I already had an experience where I was able to go to the waters and command the seas to obey me. This was another opportunity for me to obey God and do the works of God.

This is operating in our kingly authority.

Even though I have had the experience where the seas obey my command, I know that seas rage, so though I have the realization of the power that works in me, I still fight the fear of the rage☐☐☐. God help me walk in this place.

Anyway, I prayed in tongues while driving from my home to the beach. When I first got to the beach, the sun was just above the horizon, and I began to scream with joy because it was sooooo beautiful. I looked to find a spot to park. I don't know why, at 7am it was crowded at the beach, but I assume many wanted to see the sunrise as well. I immediately found a spot that I passed by, but when I went to put the car in reverse to turn into the parking spot, someone came up so aggressively behind me that I just said, "I will come back around." As I scurried to find another parking spot, I just decided to go back to the one I saw originally. Now it's time for me to pay. I'm downloading the app, and it's a big ordeal and time waster, so I missed ALL the beauty of the sunrise by the time I got everything squared away. That was OK because I was excited about putting my prayer notes in the water.

I walked along the shore and continued speaking in tongues. I told the water, "Good morning. God bless you." It is a living being, so I spoke to it. As I spoke to it, I felt like it responded with light waves against my feet. I stopped at a spot along the shore. At this spot, the water was retracted as if it was waiting for me to do something. It came forward very lightly and gently. It was not encompassing. I said, "Let the water bring forth said prayer in abundance." I put my sticky note on the water, and at first, it sat on top of the water. I thought, "Man, people are going to see that. I want the water to consume it.". Next thing you know, a wave came and consumed it. I was like, "O...k..." I put down the next sticky note and said the same thing, and a wave came and grabbed it, taking it into the waters. Then I thought, "Oh, God created it, then He spoke to the waters." The next few sticky notes, I said, "I create said prayer, and waters, bring forth said prayer in abundance." Once all the prayers were in the sea, I kept walking along the shore, praying and admiring the beauty of God's creation. I prayed for the waters because as I walked, I felt a residue on my skin. I felt like the water was still contaminated from sewer dumps in the past. I prayed that the waters be purified and that all contaminants be cleared out. Then I stopped at a spot, and something shifted—this calm sea with mild waves began to have waves back-to-back very frequently. They weren't like this previously. There was no wind. I said to God, "What is happening?" and He said, "Those are the contractions of the bringing forth of your prayers." Then the seas just got calm again. It was so amazing! As I went back to my car, this song was playing in my head called "The Heavens Are Telling." The first line says, "The heavens are telling about God's glory, what a mighty God we serve." It was a beautiful time of worship!

When travailing in intercession, one can feel the varying types of intensity while praying. At times, the prayer feels calm, and other times, it's as if we are giving birth to what we prayed for—the intensity intensifies, just as the waters did when I put my prayers in the water.

FORM

Let's revisit the Scripture that was spoken of in the above "Create" section.

Genesis 2:7 KJV
[7] And the LORD God formed man of the dust of the ground, and breathed into his nostrils the breath of life; and man became a living soul.

The word "form" in the above-referenced Scripture is yatsar in Hebrew, and it means "fashioned." I like to think of this from a modern perspective: God styled man. He fashioned him from the dirt of the earth, which is linked to a potter forming clay.

"Form" and "travail" can correlate with one another.

Let's read Psalm 90:2, which speaks of the creation of the earth and the world.

Psalm 90:2 KJV
[2] Before the mountains were brought forth, or ever thou hadst formed the earth and the world, Even from everlasting to everlasting, thou art God.

In Psalm 90:2, the words "were brought forth" come from a Hebrew word used to refer to childbirth: **yalad**. This word means to give birth or to bear, and it can also be associated with travail. You can read more about **yalad** in my book, Office of the Midwife.

The word "form" here is related to the word "moved" in Genesis 1:2. In Psalm 90:2, "form" means that God Himself travailed to bring forth the earth and the world. This word, "form," is associated with the Hebrew word chuwl, which *means to whirl, dance, or writhe.*

Writhe is a word that we don't see used frequently in the English language, but according to dictionary.com, *it means (a) make continual twisting, squirming movements or contortions of the body. (b) respond with great emotional or physical discomfort to (a violent or unpleasant feeling or thought)*

In conjunction with childbearing, when a woman is in pain as she gives birth, she squirms from the pain of the contractions. She is uncomfortable and twists and turns her body from the pain. Who would have thought that this could be considered a dance, just as the Hebrew word chuwl implies according to its definition?

One can surmise from this that when God created heaven and earth, He was in travail, and this travail involved all of Him because there was a dance to produce. I cannot say that when God travailed, He was in pain. Let's recount the judgment of Adam and Eve when they ate from the tree of the knowledge of good and evil.

Genesis 3:15-18
And I will put enmity Between you and the woman, And between your seed and her Seed; He shall bruise your head, And you shall bruise His heel." To the woman He said: **"I will greatly multiply your sorrow and your conception; In pain you shall bring forth children;** *Your desire shall be for your husband, And he shall rule over you." Then to Adam He said,*

"Because you have heeded the voice of your wife, and have eaten from the tree of which I commanded you, saying, 'You shall not eat of it': "Cursed is the ground for your sake; In toil you shall eat of it All the days of your life. Both thorns and thistles it shall bring forth for you, And you shall eat the herb of the field.

From the above Scriptures, one can see that bringing forth had no pain. The judgment given to the woman included pain in bringing forth. The toil that women now experience in bringing forth comes from the judgments placed on Adam and Eve.

HOW DOES MAN FORM AS GOD DID?

There was a scenario where one of my family members had a friend with some manner of corneal abrasion. Their eye was shaped like a cone and protruded from the natural shape of the eye. It was always dry, and this person could not see out of it. I would hold quarterly 6-hour prayer shut-ins at the leading of the Holy Spirit, and he came to one of them. Because I had a sign-up sheet for the shut-in, I knew in advance who was coming, and God had given me instructions to get dirt, spit in it, and put it on his eyes, just as Jesus did. God prompted me to review the Scripture where Jesus performed this work. It is found in John 9:1-7. Let's review the story.

John 9:1-7 KJV
*[1] And as Jesus passed by, he saw a man which was blind from his birth. [2] And his disciples asked him, saying, Master, who did sin, this man, or his parents, that he was born blind? [3] Jesus answered, **Neither hath this man sinned, nor his parents: but that the works of God should be made manifest in him. [4] I must work the works of him that sent me, while it is day**: the night cometh, when no man can work. [5] As long as I am in the world, I am the light of the world. [6] When he had thus spoken, he spat on the ground, and made clay of the spittle, and he anointed the eyes of the blind man*

with the clay, [7] and said unto him, Go, wash in the pool of Siloam, (which is by interpretation, Sent.) He went his way therefore, and washed, and came seeing.

Let's look at this portion of Scripture:
Jesus answered, "Neither hath this man sinned, nor his parents: but that the works of God should be made manifest in him. [4] I must work the works of him that sent me."

As we walk with God, we begin to come into our divine essence. We become the image AND likeness of God. As we walk with Him, He trains us to say and do what He said and did, and what He is still doing. Here we have Jesus working as the Father worked, as expressed in the "Create" section. We are kings and priests after the order of Melchizedek. As God brings us into alignment with our kingly authority and reign, He teaches us how to stand in dominion and to work the works He did.

Back to the prayer encounter I spoke about earlier: it came time to actually do what God had instructed me to do, and man, was I nervous! I was literally shaking. In spite of that, I did what the Lord asked me. I mixed water with the spit and put it on his eyes after some hours of prayer at the shut-in. I prayed for his eye along with another intercessor. As the sun came up and everyone was still at my home after the prayer, this person said, *"My eyes won't stop watering."* Honestly, I didn't know what that meant. Then this person said, *"I can see the light."* I still didn't know what that meant. Then this person explained, *"I haven't had tears or any manner of water out of this eye in quite some time. I haven't even had the ability to see light."*

This action was the "forming" of his miracle.

NIKKI GARCIA

THE ASCENT INTO TRAVAIL

Let's study travail by first having an in-depth dive through the prayer of supplication. It will all make sense as we move forward.

Let's review *1 Timothy 2:1 ESV*

First of all, then, I urge that supplications, prayers, intercessions, and thanksgivings be made for all people

This verse provides a summary of the types of offerings that can be offered to God for man.

(1)   **Supplication** falls under a request. The Bible says, "...with prayers and supplications, make your requests known to God" (Philippians 4:6-8). Supplications are emotional, heartfelt pleas before God. Why? Because pleas ARE requests, whether from the saved or unsaved. For believers in Christ, this type of plea can be used in intercession. As citizens of the Kingdom of God, we can create a petition before the Lord, and that petition can include supplications and emotional pleas on behalf of a person, place, or thing. Supplication can also be defined as an earnest or humble request.

(2)   **Prayers**
The constant thinking and intent of man: This is our priestly practice. The thinking and intent of man is incense unto God. An example of this is the account of Sodom and Gomorrah. During this time, God said that the intent of man's heart was constantly evil. And GOD saw that the wickedness of man was great in the earth and that every imagination of the thoughts of his heart was only evil continually *(Genesis 6:5)*. The will is the way of man. What do I mean? It is the direction man is currently going because of his thinking. As a man thinketh in his heart, so is he (Proverbs 23:7). Thinking is man's will on the altar; it is the sacrifice rendered. To reiterate, prayer is the will of man on the altar of God and the will of God answering heaven and earth. Prayer, often, in the Bible is known as an exchange. An exchange of what? Our will for His. It is God's

way. We seek Him, and we receive His way.

There is a way that seemeth right unto a man, but the end thereof is death *(Proverbs 14:12)*.

The word "way" in this Scripture refers to the thinking of man and the path he follows because of this thinking.

Let's look at Genesis 6:5 further.

The imagination in this Scripture is called intent. Which means a form, framing, purpose of what is framed in the mind. It is the good and bad tendency of man.

Hebrews 11:3 even iterates the aspect of framing further.

[3] Through faith we understand that the worlds were framed by the word of God, so that things which are seen were not made of things which do appear.

To this point, man can create good and evil by the words and intents of his heart; he frames his heart and intent. Think about construction for a second. When a house is being built, they lay the foundation and then begin to frame the house. This allows the home to take shape and form.

As we have hidden desires and intents in our hearts, they begin to take form through the words we speak. Just as the book of Genesis declares that God formed man in His image and likeness, the word also says that out of the abundance of the heart, the mouth speaks.

Matthew 12:34-36 KJV
[34] O generation of vipers, how can ye, being evil, speak good things? for out of the abundance of the heart the mouth speaketh. [35] A good man out of the good treasure of the heart bringeth forth good things: and an evil man out of the evil treasure bringeth forth evil things. [36] But I say unto you, That every idle word that men shall speak, they shall give account thereof in the day of judgment.

(3)   Intercession

This is from my soon-to-be-released book, "The Answer to Prayer." What is intercession? Intercession are pleadings before God. It involves vocalizing (whether in the heart or out of the mouth) an emotional plea that begins or causes us to engage in a court session associated with this outcry. This is different from prayer.

Prayer and intercession are both priestly activities, but in intercession, because my life has been a living sacrifice on the altar, I can come to God on behalf of another person or place. During this time, we commune with God and offer sacrifices on His altar.

In intercession, we advocate on behalf of someone, something, or ourselves, making an emotional plea to prevent certain things from happening.

(4)   Thanksgiving

Psalms 100:4 - 4 Enter into his gates with thanksgiving, and into his courts with praise: be thankful unto him, and bless his name.

When we speak of the Prayer of Thanksgiving, this implies that there are multiple ways we can give thanks for what we are thankful for. Giving thanks is a response to the grace that God has extended to us.

Thanksgiving can be extended for who God is and for what He has done. It can be a prayer, a song, a dance, an offering (such as a wave offering or a monetary offering), or any other type of offering unto God, including a vow and many more expressions that one or many can give unto the Lord.

Thankfulness is one of the ways we exalt God. It stands as an intersection point between our will and God's will. Thankfulness begins in the heart and can extend to a deity. It is the expression of love and purity of hope that rests on the altar to produce a byproduct of faith

THE COURTS OF HEAVEN

The concept of the Courts of Heaven comes from the revelation that God shared with Apostle Robert Henderson around 2009. To learn more about the Courts of Heaven, you can read his books. This section provides a brief introduction to the Courts of Heaven, but the insights below are drawn from my own studies. The following section includes legal terms to lay the foundation for the next chapter.

What is a plea? A plea is a request made in an urgent and emotional manner.

"He made a dramatic plea for disarmament"

I am very adamant that when God uses a word, that is what He means. Though words can be interchanged, they are not the same. Each word has a specific nature and meaning. Below are words similar to "plea," which do not change its specific meaning. This is intended to further help the reader understand what a plea is by association. Words similar to "plea" include:

(1)   appeal
(2)   entreaty
(3)   supplication
(4)   petition
(5)   prayer
(6)   request
(7)   call
(8)   solicitation
(9)   invocation
(10)   suit
(11)   imploration
(12)   adjuration

The Legal Definition of a Plea: A formal statement by or on behalf of a defendant or prisoner, stating guilt or innocence in response to a charge, offering an allegation of fact, or claiming that a point of law should apply.

"He changed his plea to not guilty"

What is the difference between a plea and a petition?

A plea is "an urgent, emotional request." A petition is "a formal request usually made by citizens to the government."

As a citizen of the Kingdom of God, supplication can intersect with intercession because it is a Pleading before the Lord to intervene in a situation, and as a Kingdom citizen of the government of God, it becomes a petition about a matter. Which is, again, a formal request made by a citizen of the Kingdom to the Kingdom of God.

Summarizing everything just explained: Supplication is an emotional plea, possibly even a plea of desperation. It is an emotional claim and/or an emotional defense before God.

It is a heartfelt petition arising from deep personal need (a sense of lack or want).

In our earthly court system, a pleading is the beginning stage of a lawsuit, where parties formally submit their claims and defenses.

Pleadings are formal documents filed with the court that state the parties' basic positions. Common pre-trial pleadings include a complaint (or petition or bill).

From this definition, we can see how, as citizens of the

Kingdom of God, our plea can intersect with intercession and become a petition in our government's court system.

Supplication is when I come before God with my side of an issue. I pour my will on the altar of God in surrender, from a place of emotional distress or outcry, on behalf of myself or another.

We see this type of prayer in 1 Samuel 1:9-19, which we will review in depth in the next chapter.

Below is a sample prayer where one would engage the Courts of Heaven and how to do so.

COURTS OF HEAVEN

The courts of heaven allow us to actually go to heaven and go before God the judge and deal with legal issues that the enemy has against us and others.

Psalms 139:16
16 Thine eyes did see my substance, yet being unperfect; and in thy book all my members were written, which in continuance were fashioned, when as yet there was none of them.

One thing to note about the Courts of Heaven is that it is not merely a method of praying; it is an entrance into the unseen realm. This means that when this type of prayer is offered, we ascend into the invisible Kingdom of Heaven. How do we step into this place? By faith.

John 14:2
2 In my Father's house are many mansions: if it were not so, I would have told you. I go to prepare a place for you.

Follow these steps to pray this type of prayer:

Step (1)

Ask that the court be convened on your behalf.

Step (2)
Present the case to the judge.

Step (3)
Repent for all manner of wrongs you have committed in association with the case you are presenting.

An example of this would be negative words you have spoken, or even actions that you or your ancestors and bloodline may have committed, whether you are aware of them or not.

Step (4)
Repent for the wrongs others have committed associated with the case for which you are repenting (according to 1 John 5:16-18).

16 If any man see his brother sin a sin which is not unto death, he shall ask, and he shall give him life for them that sin not unto death. There is a sin unto death: I do not say that he shall pray for it.

17 All unrighteousness is sin: and there is a sin not unto death.

18 We know that whosoever is born of God sinneth not; but he that is begotten of God keepeth himself, and that wicked one toucheth him not.

Step (5)
Speak the Word over the situation. What Bible verses declare God's intended purpose and promises regarding the situation?

Prophecy. If you have the ability to prophesy, speak the revealed Word of God concerning the matter.

16 If any man see his brother sin a sin which is not unto death, he shall ask, and he shall give him life for them that sin not unto death. There is a sin unto death: I do not say that he shall pray for it.
17 All unrighteousness is sin: and there is a sin not unto death.
18 We know that whosoever is born of God sinneth not; but he that is begotten of God keepeth himself, and that wicked one toucheth him not.

We must come before God in true repentance, as all of these things can and will be used to build a case against us by demon spirits in the Courts of Heaven.

The two previous steps address the accusations the enemy has against you or others.

Revelations 12:10

And I heard a loud voice saying in heaven, Now is come salvation, and strength, and the kingdom of our God, and the power of his Christ: for the accuser of our brethren is cast down, which accused them before our God day and night.

A sample prayer would look as follows:

(1) Righteous Judge, I come before You asking You to allow the courts of heaven to convene on my behalf.
(2) I present to You a case concerning this nation and human trafficking. Many souls are being taken advantage of and captured into bondage because of the sins of this nation.
(3) I enter a plea of guilty for every accusation of the enemy and repent for everything I've done against Your Word through unrighteous deeds. I ask You, Righteous Judge, for a guilty verdict to be rendered as it pertains to unrighteous bills and laws in this nation, and for human trafficking rings that have not yet been uncovered and exposed.

(4) I stand on behalf of this nation, repenting for all the wrongs of this nation. I repent for my agreement with these acts. I repent for not taking a stand in righteousness against these acts in my community.

(5) I ask You, Righteous Judge, for places for the children and people who have been abused to go, for Christian orphanages to arise, and for ministries to arise to reach impacted families and children:

- That they are provided for
- That their souls be restored
- That they can recover their life
- That they can recover their mind
- That the seed of unrighteousness doesn't destroy their ability to receive God
- That our legal system create safe houses for victims

You word says in Matthew 5:3-11

3 Blessed are the poor in spirit: for theirs is the kingdom of heaven. **4** Blessed are they that mourn: for they shall be comforted. **5** Blessed are the meek: for they shall inherit the earth. **6** Blessed are they which do hunger and thirst after righteousness: for they shall be filled. **7** Blessed are the merciful: for they shall obtain mercy. **8** Blessed are the pure in heart: for they shall see God. **9** Blessed are the peacemakers: for they shall be called the children of God. **10** Blessed are they which are persecuted for righteousness' sake: for theirs is the kingdom of heaven.**11** Blessed are ye, when men shall revile you, and persecute you, and shall say all manner of evil against you falsely, for my sake.

I ask that you avenge the unrighteous deeds in this nation.

NIKKI GARCIA

HANNAH'S PRAYER MODEL

THE PANT OF THE RIGHTEOUS

Now that we have laid the groundwork in the previous chapter, let's look at the model of prayer that Hannah prayed...

1 Samuel 1:8-18 KJV

[8] Then said Elkanah her husband to her, Hannah, why weepest thou? and why eatest thou not? and why is thy heart grieved? am not I better to thee than ten sons? [9] So Hannah rose up after they had eaten in Shiloh, and after they had drunk. Now Eli the priest sat upon a seat by a post of the temple of the LORD. [10] And she was in bitterness of soul, and prayed unto the LORD, and wept sore. Bitterness of soul (crying, weeping, and not eating)[11] And she vowed a vow, and said, O LORD of hosts, if thou wilt indeed look on the affliction of thine handmaid, and remember me, and not forget thine handmaid, but wilt give unto thine handmaid a man child, then I will give him unto the LORD all the days of his life, and there shall no razor come upon his head. [12] And it came to pass, as she continued praying before the LORD, that Eli marked her mouth. [13] Now Hannah, she spake in her heart; only her lips moved, but her voice was not heard: therefore Eli thought she had been drunken. [14] And Eli said unto her, How long wilt thou be drunken? put away thy wine from thee.[15] And Hannah answered and said, No, my lord, I am a woman of a sorrowful spirit: I have drunk neither wine nor strong drink, but have poured out my soul before the LORD. [16] Count not thine handmaid for a daughter of Belial: for out of the abundance of my complaint and grief have I spoken hitherto. [17] Then Eli answered and said, Go in peace: and the God of Israel grant thee thy petition that thou hast asked of him.
[18] And she said, Let thine handmaid find grace in thy sight. So the woman went her way, and did eat, and her countenance was no more sad.

Before we dive into the spiritual explanation of Hannah's travail, I want to give a small commentary about the word "travail." I want to focus on the Prefix and Suffix.

The prefix is "tra," which comes from the prefix "trans," meaning "across." This indicates that you go from one state of being to another state of being.

The suffix "vail" means humility; to let sink lower or to take off one's hat in submission.

Focusing on the prefix "tra," we see this prefix in words like "transitive" and "traverse." It is a prefix that indicates movement. Hannah traversed through travail in her prayer. She had multiple types of prayers in the prayer model that Hannah traversed.

Now let's digest and meditate on all that we just read.

[8] Then said Elkanah her husband to her, Hannah, why weepest thou? and why eatest thou not? and why is thy heart grieved? am not I better to thee than ten sons?

Verse 8: Reveals Hannah's current state of being. Hannah's heart was grieved.

[9] So Hannah rose up after they had eaten in Shiloh, and after they had drunk. Now Eli the priest sat upon a seat by a post of the temple of the LORD.

Verse 9: Let's observe one thing about Hannah in this verse: Hannah rose up. In the previous verses of this chapter, the Bible exclaims that Hannah was in bitterness of soul, meaning the pain of her situation caused her to arise and do something. The pain of her soul caused her to enter into travail. As we explore this chapter, we will see that the pain in her soul caused her to birth in the spirit. Travail has painful and laborious effort associated with it. Here, one can recognize that the natural and the supernatural are coming together, and the pain in her soul is labor in the spirit.

Eli was sitting in his place of authority as a high priest. The high priest's job was to atone for sin. They were the only ones who went once a year to the Holy of Holies to atone for the sins of the people.

Hannah goes through the door where Eli is sitting. She literally walked through the door where a gatekeeper sat. She went through the door of atonement. She walked through the blood. Her sin(s) were atoned for when she walked through the door. When she transitioned through the door, Eli possessed the authority to atone for her sin(s).

Further confirmation of this can be found in One for Israel:

"Later in the book of Judges, another barren woman appeals to the high priest, Eli, who was at the doorway of the temple (1 Samuel 1:9). Another mother of a transition follows as God brings Samuel onto the scene, who would usher in the era of the kings after the time of the judges." https://www.oneforisrael.org/bible-based-teaching-from-israel/open-doors-portals-and-gateways-in-the-bible/

Let me point out the word "transition" in the above statement. We have the prefix "tra" yet again. As Hannah is **tra**versing through prayer, she is **tra**nsitioning from one state of being to another. As we continue reading, we will further dissect Hannah's prayer model. We can also observe that this marked the birth of a new era of kings. Her pregnancy was both prophetic and necessary.

[10] And she was in bitterness of soul, and prayed unto the LORD, and wept sore.

Bitterness of soul (crying, weeping, and not eating)

Verse 10 - Says that Hannah was in bitterness of soul and prayed. Hannah entered into a plea before God's court. This prayer was an emotional plea before God—a plea of desperation.

[11] And she vowed a vow, and said, O LORD of hosts, if thou wilt indeed look on the affliction of thine handmaid, and remember me, and not forget thine handmaid, but wilt give unto thine handmaid a man child, then I will give him unto the LORD all the days of his life, and there shall no razor come upon his head.

Verse 11 - Within her plea, she makes a covenant with God by making a vow before Him, saying that if He would give her a son, she would give him back to God and let no razor come to his head. She then brings the prayer of remembrance before Him.

What is the prayer of remembrance? The prayer of remembrance in Hebrew is called "Zakar." In English, this means to bring something to the forefront of one's mind, but in Hebrew, Zakar, according to Chad Bird, a Jewish scholar, means that God is actively seeking to help someone; remembrance translated into action. It is to act on their behalf, to be with them in mercy and compassion in His remembrance of them.

She asked Him to look. Look at what? The affliction of His handmaiden. A handmaiden was considered someone who does His will. Think of the tabernacle, with the outer courts, the inner courts, and the Holy of Holies. Now think of a court proceeding. Now read what she did: she put herself on the altar in humility (the suffix "-vail"). She made a covenant, which was an exchange on the altar of God: "If You give me a man-child, I will give him back to You." She made a supplication or request for God to remember her worship (the affliction of His handmaiden).

[12] And it came to pass, as she continued praying before the LORD, that Eli marked her mouth.
[13] Now Hannah, she spake in her heart; only her lips moved, but her voice was not heard: therefore Eli thought she had been drunken.

Verses 12-13: Let's first review *Romans 8:26-27*

26 *Likewise the Spirit also helpeth our infirmities: for we know not what we should pray for as we ought: but the Spirit itself maketh intercession for us with groanings which cannot be uttered.*

27 *And he that searcheth the hearts knoweth what is the mind of the Spirit, because he maketh intercession for the saints according to the will of God.*

Observing Hannah and what the Bible says in verses 12 and 13, she prayed in her heart, and her lips moved, but no voice was heard. I used to think this meant that the Holy Spirit would moan and groan through you in accordance with the birthing pains associated with the prayer of travail, which He will do at times. But what about the times when you can't express the emotional desperation or anguish your soul is experiencing, and nothing verbal can be spoken? The Holy Spirit interprets the anguish of your soul and mind and the intent of your heart.

To further confirm this, the book Travail to Prevail: A Key to Experiencing the Heart of God by Joseph Mattera states:

"Paul is not talking about a verbal language, but "groanings".

This word in Greek is "stenagmos", which translates as, to groan, to sigh, prayers to God expressed inarticulately; the sighing person is in distress. Surely, this does not necessarily reflect a "prayer language like tongues" but a prayer expressed by gut-level moans and groans that accurately describe the desperate condition of a human heart. God must be pleased with this type of prayer because it states that when someone is in this kind of deep intercession, it is actually the Holy Spirit praying inside of them" (Mattera, p. 36).

The Word of God confirms this in Romans 8:26-28 (MSG): "**26-28** Meanwhile, the moment we get tired in the waiting, God's Spirit is right alongside helping us along. If we don't know how or what to pray, it doesn't matter. He does our praying in and for us, making prayer out of our **wordless sighs, our aching groans.** He knows us far better than we know ourselves, knows our pregnant condition, and keeps us present before God. That's why we can be so sure that every detail in our lives of love for God is worked into something good."

This is truly the **Pant of the Righteous**. When you cannot utter a word and groans are so deep that the only thing that comes out of your mouth is breath. The pant is the crying out for living waters to come forth. Have you ever watched an animal pant when they are thirsty? Their tongue hangs out in desperation for water. There is even a pant that comes when there is dire thirst. It is what happens before waters break forth when a woman is conceiving. The pant before is the hunger and announcement of death (we'll talk about this in a later chapter) and the coming of the breaking of waters.

We observed in an earlier chapter, The Travail of God the

Father, how He writhed at creation. He moved and twisted or whirled with great emotional or physical discomfort. Hannah endured the same type of emotional anguish and discomfort.

This is definitely a different type of prayer on the altar of God, extending into the anguish of the soul. The only thing being expelled is the ruach of God. What is the ruach of God? In the book of Genesis, there is a scripture that talks about God breathing into the nostrils of man, and man became a living soul. That breath of life is the very thing being expelled through the mouth of man.

Genesis 2:7
And the Lord God formed man of the dust of the ground, and breathed into his nostrils the breath of life; and man became a living soul.

The breath of life in Genesis 2:7 is the word "ruach." This breath, however, correlates with the anguish of the soul. Often, when this occurs, it can be painful to expel through the mouth because of the emotional outcry and pain being expressed through the breath.

Let's continue dissecting the passage.

[17] Then Eli answered and said, Go in peace: and the God of Israel grant thee thy petition that thou hast asked of him.

Verse 17: Eli sees her and misjudges the situation. Once Hannah explains that she is in bitterness of soul and not drunk, Eli, a representative of God, says, **"Go in peace, and the God of Israel grant thee thy petition that thou hast asked of Him."**

The beauty in this story is when Hannah came out of self and stopped wanting to have a son for self and gave her son for the purpose and the intent of God's heart and the Kingdom of God, the shift happened.

She traversed through the courts of God. The Scripture affirms this by stating, "the God of Israel grant thee thy petition." Hannah left in a different state of being, meaning that travail had taken place.

This is travail: to go from one state of being to another.

She traversed through multiple types of prayers and supplications before the Lord. She labored in prayer before the God of heaven and earth and birthed forth the manifested result of her travail.

Let's now read *1 Samuel 1:19-20 KJV*

[19] And they rose up in the morning early, and worshipped before the LORD, and returned, and came to their house to Ramah: and Elkanah knew Hannah his wife; and the LORD remembered her. [20] Wherefore it came to pass, when the time was come about after Hannah had conceived, that she bare a son, and called his name Samuel, saying, Because I have asked him of the LORD.

Verse 19: Let's observe how Hannah and Elkanah went up and worshiped the Lord. This further confirms that Hannah was God's handmaiden, looking to do His will. The worship offered to the Lord continued into the matrimony of husband and wife, and the prayer of remembrance that Hannah prayed before is now answered in intimacy—twofold, spiritually and naturally. Hannah conceived and bore a son, naming him Samuel.

God was able to use Samuel to be His priest, to do away with the old priestly regime, to enforce God's holiness, and to bring forth a new king. It was a type and shadow of kings and priests.

God will use your pain, which is your travail, to birth His will on earth.

The last thing I want to point out in Hannah's prayer model is the Prayer of Thanksgiving.

This is found in *1 Samuel 2:1-10 KJV*

[1] And Hannah prayed, and said, My heart rejoiceth in the LORD, Mine horn is exalted in the LORD: My mouth is enlarged over mine enemies; Because I rejoice in thy salvation. [2] There is none holy as the LORD: For there is none beside thee: Neither is there any rock like our God. [3] Talk no more so exceeding proudly; Let not arrogancy come out of your mouth: For the LORD is a God of knowledge, And by him actions are weighed. [4] The bows of the mighty men are broken, And they that stumbled are girded with strength. [5] They that were full have hired out themselves for bread; And they that were hungry ceased: So that the barren hath born seven; And she that hath many children is waxed feeble. [6] The LORD killeth, and maketh alive: He bringeth down to the grave, and bringeth up. [7] The LORD maketh poor, and maketh rich: He bringeth low, and lifteth up. [8] He raiseth up the poor out of the dust, And lifteth up the beggar from the dunghill, To set them among princes, And to make them inherit the throne of glory: For the pillars of the earth are the LORD's, And he hath set the world upon them. [9] He will keep the feet of his saints, And the wicked shall be silent in darkness; For by strength shall no man prevail. [10] The adversaries of the LORD shall be broken to pieces; Out of heaven shall he thunder upon them: The LORD shall judge the ends of the earth; And he shall give strength unto his king, And exalt the horn of his anointed.

Hannah gave thanks for what He had done. One of the things

God showed me about Thanksgiving is the following:

Let's read **Nehemiah 12:8**:

Moreover the Levites: Jeshua, Binnui, Kadmiel, Sherebiah, Judah, and Mattaniah, which was over the thanksgiving, he and his brethren.

The beauty of this Scripture is that it shows how the priest managed the thanksgiving. This type of offering went through the priest. The importance of this is also seen in the Bible through the passage about the ten lepers.

Luke 17:11-19 KJV
[11] And it came to pass, as he went to Jerusalem, that he passed through the midst of Samaria and Galilee. [12] And as he entered into a certain village, there met him ten men that were lepers, which stood afar off: [13] and they lifted up their voices, and said, Jesus, Master, have mercy on us. [14] And when he saw them, he said unto them, Go shew yourselves unto the priests. And it came to pass, that, as they went, they were cleansed. [15] And one of them, when he saw that he was healed, turned back, and with a loud voice glorified God, [16] and fell down on his face at his feet, giving him thanks: and he was a Samaritan. [17] And Jesus answering said, Were there not ten cleansed? but where are the nine? [18] There are not found that returned to give glory to God, save this stranger. [19] And he said unto him, Arise, go thy way: thy faith hath made thee whole.

It was customary to show yourself to the priest when you had leprosy, and the priest would determine whether or not you could return to society.

According to the Virtual Jewish Library,

"The priest was called in to inspect the affliction. If "leprosy" was only suspected but not certain, the priest imposed a seven-day quarantine. At the end of this period, the afflicted was examined again, and if no further degeneration was apparent he was isolated for another week, after which he could be pronounced healed. The priest, however, did nothing to promote the cure. His rituals were performed only after the disease had passed. It was the responsibility of the afflicted himself to pray." https://www.jewishvirtuallibrary.org/leprosy

Back to the passage in Luke: the other lepers were cleansed as they went, but because of the one who came back and gave thanks, Jesus now walked in the role of the priest from the very offering that person brought. In return for the man pouring out upon the altar an offering of thanksgiving, God's response was that the man was made whole.

In light of this understanding, let's stop and create an altar of thanksgiving.

We take this moment in time to create an altar thanking God for the privilege of being able to understand His word in a new dimension. We thank Him for revealing His goodness to us and for shining and illuminating our understanding. May this dimension of travail never be closed to us, but may it remain a memorial; for the spirit of understanding has visited us. May our hearts continue to grow in this understanding. Thank You, Elohim, for You are great, and no one can touch us as You do. To God be all the glory. Amen and Amen!

One last thing to observe is that God blessed Hannah with 7 children. The number 7 is the number of perfection and fulfillment. Through Hannah's travail, God perfected her womb and fulfilled His word.

THE PASSION OF CHRIST

THE PANT OF REDEMPTION AND KINGDOM

We have reviewed the travail of God and the travail of the righteous in previous chapters. Let's begin this chapter by taking a deeper look into the definition of travail. In doing this, I may be reiterating some things, but I want to ensure that I am connecting the dots. What is travail?

Travail, by definition, is a painful or laborious effort.

Travailing is laboring in prayer and related faith actions about a matter. This action is laborious, meaning you will labor. It can be a physical manifestation exhibiting strong similarities to a woman laboring until the manifested result(s) is/are birthed forth. We reviewed this in Hannah's prayer model.

RECOGNIZING WHEN TRAVAIL IS UPON YOU

The symptoms of travail include:

- Extreme Burdens
- Your soul may feel pain
- Anxiety
- Weeping
- Feeling a person's burden(s) and knowing their thought(s)
- Knots in your belly
- Know the extreme displeasure or deep feelings of God about a situation
- Hard to pray to get words out and articulate what you're feeling

Let me share an example of this. Many times, while in prayer, I have had a very hard time praying for a particular issue (an extreme burden) or in a particular prayer setting (a hard atmosphere: hearts that are not open to God's Spirit and His will for the setting). So much so, that I have had to bend over to get the words out. There were even times when I had to sit on the floor to pray with great intensity. I had one scenario, while at church interceding, where by the time I finished praying, my stomach hurt for days. My abdominal muscles, my back—everything was hurting because of the intensity of the burden that came upon me as I prayed. It felt like I had an intense workout.

Let me explain that. There are times when you pray for a specific topic, purpose, or matter, and it becomes hard to pray. The words are hard to say. To get them out makes you feel weak. In this type of instance, you are experiencing travail. For the longest time, I thought I was in warfare and needed to press to break through, but I have come to learn through years of prayer and intercession that this is the **extreme burden** of the prayer being prayed.

2 Thess 3:8 confirms this.

Neither did we eat any man's bread for nought; but wrought with labour and travail night and day, that we might not be chargeable to any of you:

PASSION 1: THE TRAVAIL OF REDEMPTION

Let's recount Jesus in the Garden of Gethsemane

Matthew 26:36-38 KJV
[36] Then cometh Jesus with them unto a place called Gethsemane, and saith unto the disciples, Sit ye here, while I go and pray yonder. [37] And he took with him Peter and the two sons of Zebedee, and began to be sorrowful and very

heavy. [38] Then saith he unto them, My soul is exceeding sorrowful, even unto death: tarry ye here, and watch with me.

The aforementioned verses start similarly to the prayer of Hannah. The Bible says that "Hannah was in bitterness of soul." We see where Jesus' soul was sorrowful even unto death.

It wasn't the same manner of agony physically, but they both encountered a death of "self." They both experienced agony in their souls.

Matthew 26:39-45 KJV
39 And he went a little farther, and fell on his face, and prayed, saying, O my Father, if it be possible, let this cup pass from me: nevertheless not as I will, but as thou wilt. 40 And he cometh unto the disciples, and findeth them asleep, and saith unto Peter, What, could ye not watch with me one hour? 41 Watch and pray, that ye enter not into temptation: the spirit indeed is willing, but the flesh is weak. 42 He went away again the second time, and prayed, saying, O my Father, if this cup may not pass away from me, except I drink it, thy will be done. 43 And he came and found them asleep again: for their eyes were heavy. 44 And he left them, and went away again, and prayed the third time, saying the same words. 45 Then cometh he to his disciples, and saith unto them, Sleep on now, and take your rest: behold, the hour is at hand, and the Son of man is betrayed into the hands of sinners.

Jesus prayed 3 times that this cup be taken from him. Can you imagine knowing what was going to happen and maybe even not to the full extent but to some extent? What if Jesus even knew the full extent? I can guarantee you that the agony of knowing and the pain of experiencing are two totally different matters.

Luke describes it this way in 22:44

And being in an agony he prayed more earnestly: and his sweat was as it were great drops of blood falling down to the ground.

There are a few things I want to point out about what we just read.

(1)   He prayed more earnestly. That word "earnestly," ektenesteron, in Greek means more intently. We spoke earlier in Chapter 2 about the intentions of man. These intentions are connected to action. This prayer was connected to the intention of Jesus to bear the cross at Calvary. It was a prayer of hyper-focus.

(2)   This is an altar. Gethsemane was an altar. How can you tell? There is always a death. Dead things are rendered on the altar. When Jesus said, "Nevertheless, not as I will but as You will," His will (self) had to die. The other way you can tell this was an altar is that the Bible says, "sweat was as it were great drops of blood falling to the ground." Strong's Concordance likens this to blood drops or blood clots.

Whether it was the water of His body turned into blood, just like in the times with Pharaoh, or if it was blood clots where the body was trying to rush to heal itself from the sin that Jesus was already beginning to carry in His body, the wounding started way before the Garden of Gethsemane. The garden was just the manifestation of the wounding that Jesus had already endured. The travail of Calvary happened as Jesus taught the gospel.

We can observe this in **Luke 20:1-2 KJV**

[1] And it came to pass, that on one of those days, as he taught the people in the temple, and preached the gospel, the chief priests and the scribes came upon him with the elders, [2] and spake unto him, saying, Tell us, by what authority doest thou these things? or who is he that gave thee this authority?

We can read about the wounding of the soul and travail of the gospel by reading this parable:

Luke 20:9-16 KJV
[9] Then began he to speak to the people this parable; A certain man planted a vineyard, and let it forth to husbandmen, and went into a far country for a long time. [10] And at the season he sent a servant to the husbandmen, that they should give him of the fruit of the vineyard: but the husbandmen beat him, and sent him away empty. [11] And again he sent another servant: and they beat him also, and entreated him shamefully, and sent him away empty. [12] And again he sent a third: and they wounded him also, and cast him out. [13] Then said the lord of the vineyard, What shall I do? I will send my beloved son: it may be they will reverence him when they see him. [14] But when the husbandmen saw him, they reasoned among themselves, saying, This is the heir: come, let us kill him, that the inheritance may be our's. [15] So they cast him out of the vineyard, and killed him. What therefore shall the lord of the vineyard do unto them? [16] He shall come and destroy these husbandmen, and shall give the vineyard to others. And when they heard it, they said, God forbid.

From the previous passage, you can observe that the things people were doing against Jesus were transgressions. Jesus was already enduring wounds from the transgressions made against Him. As Jesus was in the Garden of Gethsemane, blood was coming out of the wounds He already had in His body from the transgressions of man. Another way to look at this is that the soul of man was wounding the soul of Jesus. I was speaking about this with my sister, and she brought up the point that through man's carnal thinking, even though Jesus, the Word, was before them, the Word was unrecognizable. The condition of their souls caused them to perceive the Word (Jesus) incorrectly. Just as they beat Him until He was unrecognizable on the outside, the same thing was happening on the inside concerning man's soul and how they came against His soul.

The blood poured out of Jesus from the wounds inflicted by the soul of man and how man perceived the Word.

There are many events leading up to the cross that can exponentially express the travail of that day but I want to bring out one specific one to tie in with the previous point.

John 19:34
But one of the soldiers with a spear pierced his side, and forthwith came there out blood and water.

I was listening to a song that says, "You got wonder-working power pouring out of your sides." I thought to myself, how does that happen? What does that mean? I received, what I call an immediate power punch, which is a quickening of the Spirit of the Lord. Let's speak briefly about quickening.

1 Corinthians 15:45
And so it is written, The first man Adam was made a living soul; the last Adam was made a quickening spirit.

I just want to point out that "quickening" can also be defined as the first time a pregnant person feels their fetus move in the uterus. God will impregnate us with revelation from on high.

Back to my point, I immediately began to think of when God created the woman in the garden.

God took the rib from the man's side and put it into the woman. The woman gives birth. The blood and water from Jesus' side symbolize God taking the punishment for the judgment rendered to woman concerning conception from her disobedience in the garden. God was redeeming man from the curse associated with how man conceived. The blood and water from the side were about conception.

The blood represents DNA, which comes from the Father. In an earlier chapter, I spoke about how the Spirit hovered over the waters. This is indicative of conception—God birthed out of the waters. In essence, God was dealing with the DNA of man and restoring it back to Himself so that man can be made in His image. The thrust by the soldier into His side was about the recovery of man's DNA.

Now that God has dealt with conception, He can have a purified bloodline, and this is how we can now address generational curses.

It is death that qualifies you to experience a resurrection. If we reflect on the various baptisms, there is always a surrender of the will, which represents a new level of surrender to God. In water baptism, a person goes under the water, signifying death and burial, and comes up, which represents resurrection. When receiving Christ, one must confess with their mouth and believe in their heart. This is another way of saying, "nevertheless, not what I will, but I make You Lord over my life" and it is what God wills. All places of surrender require a new sacrifice; that sacrifice comes with the travail of birthing something new, which includes suffering and affliction of some kind. This is what makes it an altar before God—it is a costly sacrifice.

Galatians 2:20
20 I am crucified with Christ: nevertheless I live; yet not I, but Christ liveth in me: and the life which I now live in the flesh I live by the faith of the Son of God, who loved me, and gave himself for me.

That suffering may be test(s) and trial(s) because God always tests us when there is going to be a release of any kind.

Exodus 16:4 - *Then said the Lord unto Moses, Behold, I will rain bread from heaven for you; and the people shall go out and gather a certain rate every day, that I may prove them, whether they will walk in my law, or not.*

There will also be testing that comes as a result of the accusations of the enemy. We see this in **Job 1:6-12**.

6 Now there was a day when the sons of God came to present themselves before the Lord, and Satan came also among them. 7 And the Lord said unto Satan, Whence comest thou? Then Satan answered the Lord, and said, From going to and fro in the earth, and from walking up and down in it. 8 And the Lord said unto Satan, Hast thou considered my servant Job, that there is none like him in the earth, a perfect and an upright man, one that feareth God, and escheweth evil? 9 Then Satan answered the Lord, and said, Doth Job fear God for nought? 10 Hast not thou made an hedge about him, and about his house, and about all that he hath on every side? thou hast blessed the work of his hands, and his substance is increased in the land. 11 But put forth thine hand now, and touch all that he hath, and he will curse thee to thy face. 12 And the Lord said unto Satan, Behold, all that he hath is in thy power; only upon himself put not forth thine hand. So Satan went forth from the presence of the

This is how you begin to have new wineskins. It is the process of shedding the old and coming into the new. Matt 9:17

What do you think the sacrificial lamb means? It meant the travailing of the Messiah to give birth to the redemption of mankind.

In travail, you may experience great anguish. Moanings and groanings that cannot be uttered.

Romans 8:26 *Likewise the Spirit also helpeth our infirmities: for we know not what we should pray for as we ought: but the Spirit itself maketh intercession for us with groanings which cannot be uttered.*

Sacrifices that require you to die so that a person or situation can cross into a new place. When this occurs, things are being established. Resurrection and ascension can happen, and consequently, things are conferred. "Conferred" means to grant or bestow (a title, degree, benefit, or right).

Through the process of travail, the very person or thing you are praying about is conferred to you.

PASSION 2: THE TRAVAIL OF SONS

Another passion of Jesus' travail was for sons to be birthed.

Isaiah 66:7-8

"Before she travailed, she brought forth; Before her pain came, she gave birth to a boy. "Who has heard such a thing? Who has seen such things? Can a land be born in one day? Can a nation be brought forth all at once? As soon as Zion travailed, she also brought forth her sons.

Now Hanna's travail was for a son and when she travailed, she birthed forth a son but Jesus' travail was different. His travail was for the redemption of mankind and His travail birthed forth sons.

Sonship comes out of a relationship with God. As we are faithful in pursuit of Him, God begins to welcome us into the place of fellowship and communion, leading us to follow Him. In the Bible, as Jesus walked the earth, He would often say, "Follow me." That is a very involved statement because, innately, we have been created to imitate. We imitate any and all things that influence us. However, we have this nature because we were created to imitate God. We must train ourselves to stop following everything else and follow Him. This is how we are led by God. **John 5:19** says it this way:

"Then answered Jesus and said unto them, Verily, verily, I say unto you, The Son can do nothing of himself, but what he seeth the Father do: for what things soever he doeth, these also doeth the Son likewise."

The travail of sonship is one of great expectation. If we are in expectation, we are in hope of the unseen thing—something that has yet to be birthed. We stand in joyful waiting because we know we will see our hope manifest in the seen realm.

Romans 8:19-28 KJV
19 For the earnest expectation of the creature waiteth for the manifestation of the sons of God. 20 For the creature was made subject to vanity, not willingly, but by reason of him who hath subjected the same in hope, 21 Because the creature itself also shall be delivered from the bondage of corruption into the glorious liberty of the children of God. 22 For we know that the

whole creation groaneth and travaileth in pain together until now. 23 And not only they, but ourselves also, which have the firstfruits of the Spirit, even we ourselves groan within ourselves, waiting for the adoption, to wit, the redemption of our body. 24 For we are saved by hope: but hope that is seen is not hope: for what a man seeth, why doth he yet hope for? 25 But if we hope for that we see not, then do we with patience wait for it. 26 Likewise the Spirit also helpeth our infirmities: for we know not what we should pray for as we ought: but the Spirit itself maketh intercession for us with groanings which cannot be uttered. 27 And he that searcheth the hearts knoweth what is the mind of the Spirit, because he maketh intercession for the saints according to the will of God. 28 And we know that all things work together for good to them that love God, to them who are the called according to his purpose.

Ultimately, all of creation is travailing for the manifestation of the maturing of the sons of God. Creation travails for sonship. Sonship is necessary because it brings us to the place of being an heir. We are heirs of God, and we are joint heirs with Christ.

Romans 8:17
"And if children, then heirs; heirs of God, and joint-heirs with Christ; if so be that we suffer with him, that we may be also glorified together."

When you operate as an heir, you are now possessing the enforcement of the benefit of the death of the Savior and possessing the kingship of our divine nature. Through the suffering and work of travail, we are glorified together, which is the process of coming into our divinity.

PASSION 3: THE TRAVAIL OF KINGDOM

One of the ultimate passions of Jesus' travail was to restore the Government of God on earth in which man gave over the enemy in the garden.

When the disciples asked Jesus how to pray, He gave them the "Our Father's Prayer". Let's review, *Matthew 6:9-13*

9 After this manner therefore pray ye: Our Father which art in heaven, Hallowed be thy name. 10 Thy kingdom come, Thy will be done in earth, as it is in heaven. 11 Give us this day our daily bread. 12 And forgive us our debts, as we forgive our debtors. 13 And lead us not into temptation, but deliver us from evil: For thine is the kingdom, and the power, and the glory, for ever. Amen.

To summarize these 5 verses, as I see and perceive them, is explained below.

Vs. 9: This prayer begins with worship of God. His name is hallowed, meaning it is holy and revered as such. As the prayer progresses, it progresses into praying that the Kingdom of God comes to earth.

Vs. 10: Jesus told the disciples to pray that the dominion of God comes to earth, and when it does, that the earth would fulfill or manifest the will of God. This is another way of saying, "Let God's will come."

Vs. 11: Out of God's Kingdom and His will comes everything we need.

Vs. 12: Let us live peaceably among one another.

Vs. 13: Let us not be lured away from this Kingdom by the evils and deceptions of the enemy, because God has given us power over the enemy. Everything is the Lord's. It all belongs to Him.

God has a government. We are citizens of that government. Everything belongs to God because the Kingdom is the King's domain. Everything belongs to God because He created it.

The Travail of the Kingdom is:

To rule as God, and the only way you rule as God is if you rule within what God states is yours within His domain.

As citizens of this wonderful Kingdom, we check-in/consult with the King and bring His will on earth from that check-in as mentioned before but this comes with great travail and travail includes persecution.

10 Then said he unto them, Nation shall rise against nation, and kingdom against kingdom: 11 And great earthquakes shall be in divers places, and famines, and pestilences; and fearful sights and great signs shall there be from heaven. 12 But before all these, they shall lay their hands on you, and persecute you, delivering you up to the synagogues, and into prisons, being brought before kings and rulers for my name's sake. 13 And it shall turn to you for a testimony. 14 Settle it therefore in your hearts, not to meditate before what ye shall answer: 15 For I will give you a mouth and wisdom, which all your adversaries shall not be able to gainsay nor resist. 16 And ye shall be betrayed both by parents, and brethren, and kinsfolks, and friends; and some of you shall they cause to be put to death. 17 And ye shall be hated of all men for my name's sake. 18 But there shall not an hair of your head perish. 19 In your patience possess ye your souls. 20 And when ye shall see Jerusalem compassed with armies, then know that the desolation thereof is nigh. 21 Then let them which are in Judaea flee to the mountains; and let them which are in the midst of it depart out; and let not them that are in the countries enter thereinto. 22 For these be the days of vengeance, that all things which are written may be fulfilled. 23 But woe unto them that are with child, and to them that give suck, in those days! for there shall be great distress in the land, and wrath upon this people. 24 And they shall fall by the edge of the sword, and shall be led away captive into all nations: and Jerusalem shall be trodden down of the Gentiles, until the times of the Gentiles be fulfilled. 25 And there shall be signs in the sun, and in the moon, and in the stars; and upon the earth distress of nations, with perplexity; the sea and the waves roaring; 26 Men's hearts failing them for fear, and for looking after those things which are coming on the earth: for the powers of heaven shall be shaken. 27 And then shall they see the Son of man coming in a cloud with power and great glory. 28 And when these things begin to come to pass, then look up, and lift up your heads; for your redemption draweth nigh.

Finally, there is a war that has been raging for a very long time and this war is between two Kingdoms, the kingdom of hell and the Kingdom of God. Walking in accordance with God's Kingdom isn't easy but it is the pant of the earth and the pant of the government of God; that man takes its rightful place and reigns as kings. That man possesses its souls. May we continue in travail until Christ be formed in us and His Kingdom come on earth as it is heaven.

NIKKI GARCIA

THE IMPARTATION OF TRAVAIL

PROCLAMATION OF KINGDOM & IMPARTATION OF TRAVAIL

In the year of our Lord twenty twenty _____, I am charged this day to follow the King's directives and to give my life to establish the Kingdom of God on earth as it is in heaven. This charge doesn't come merely to vow words that are nice or flattering. A Kingdom has been conferred unto me, and it is now time to be violent against injustice, to take by force first my community, my state, my nation, and the uttermost parts of the world. I will not be slack concerning this weighty task, but I will fulfill the charge of the King with fear and trembling.

It is my duty to withstand the evil one, as all power has been given unto me over all the power of the enemy. On this day, I stand as the elect of God, understanding that it is my right and privilege to be a defender and guardian of this earth. I will reign with Christ and be the mediator between God and the matters of His courts.

May the mandate and passion of Christ be the intrinsic force that catapults me into viewing the importance of my commitment to God the Father, Son, and Holy Ghost.

I hereby decree a new thrust, wind, advancement, and faith—that You breathe a new breath of "fire life" into me. That my existence will not be one of mediocrity but one of impact and force, resisting the schemes, plots, and ploys of the enemy. My days of standing on the sidelines are OVER. I have a charge to keep and a God to glorify. Revive me in my prayer places; revive me in every area of my life, that I may live in a place of purposeful direction.

I pray, Lord, for the gift of travail. I ask that this gift be imparted unto me. I give my womb to You. May every word I have read be the seed. May it billow into my womb and cause the birthing of a new type and way. I receive the impartation of travail. Brood over me with Your Spirit and birth me forth as a travailing intercessor, O God of heaven.

Now, lift up a loud voice in praise and reception.

God, establish Your word to be so, in Jesus' name. Amen!

TRAVAIL

PRAYER OF SALVATION

Lord God, I am a sinner, and I need You in my life. I ask for forgiveness for all my sins. I confess that Jesus Christ is Lord! I believe in my heart that He is the Son of God and that God raised Him from the dead. Now, Lord, I ask You to come into my heart. Live within me. Dwell within me. My life is no longer my own; I give it to You. I renounce and denounce Satan and his operation in my life, and I give You complete control!

If you said this prayer and meant it—which I know you did—then you are now saved!

Let us know you said this prayer by sending an email to: info@kingdomgirlnikki.com

ABOUT THE AUTHOR

Nikki Garcia received salvation and the baptism of the Holy Ghost at a very young age. She is a prophet of God with a mandate to teach and train the bride of Christ about prayer and intercession. She fulfills this mandate through her ministry, Nikki Garcia Ministries. Nikki also operates in the realm of business, possessing a Bachelor of Science in Computer Information Systems and currently pursuing a degree in Prophetic Science. She is also the CEO of Shine Global, LLC.

Nikki is the wife of Alex Garcia and the mother of four beautiful children: Jeremiah, Angelica, Sara, and Zoa.

www.ingramcontent.com/pod-product-compliance
Lightning Source LLC
Chambersburg PA
CBHW060427090426
42734CB00011B/2481